Time-In

When **Time-Out** Doesn't Work

Parents' Choice Approval
1999 Award

Time-In

When **Time-Out** Doesn't Work

Jean Illsley Clarke

ILLUSTRATED BY CARY PILLO

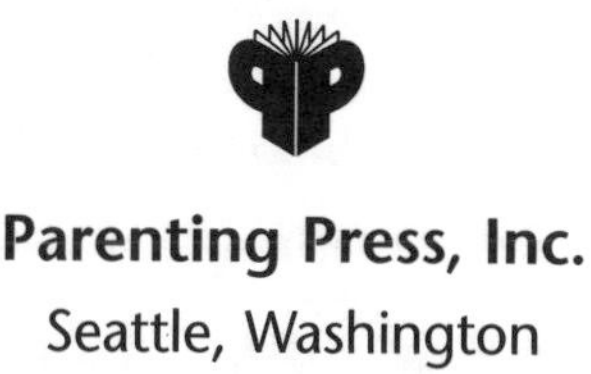

Parenting Press, Inc.

Seattle, Washington

Dedication

To all parents who have been frustrated
when discipline didn't seem to work

Designed by Magrit Baurecht Design
Printed in the United States of America

Library of Congress Cataloguing-in-Publication Data
Clarke, Jean Illsley,
Time-in : when time-out doesn't work
Jean Illsley Clarke : illustrated by Cary Pillo.
p. cm.
Includes bibliographical references and index.
ISBN 1-884734-28-6 (pbk.)
ISBN 1-884734-29-4 (lib. bdg.)
1. Child rearing. 2. Discipline of children. I. Title.
HQ769.C6133 1999
649' .64--dc21 98-37158

Parenting Press, Inc.
P.O. Box 75267
Seattle, WA 98175
www.ParentingPress.com

Contents

Acknowledgments

Many people contributed to the development of this book. I am grateful to all the people who read, tested, and offered early suggestions about this material. I especially thank Mary Sheedy Kurcinka, Joan Comeau, Barbara Kobe, Beth Brekke, Diane Wagenhals, Carole and Ann Gesme, and Carolyn Fuchs. Also the parenting class at Wisconsin Indian Head Technical College for reminding me that parents need help with their own anger.

I especially appreciate Elizabeth Crary's inspiration that my newsletter about Time-In should be the core of this book.

For challenging conversations about the need for connecting as a positive part of discipline, I thank Connie Dawson, Eveline Goodall, Laurie Kanyer, and Sandy Keiser.

I thank the many people who read the manuscript and offered valuable insights: Stacia Ikpe, Lucy DiGiovenale, Nat Houtz, Linda R. Hughes, M.D., Janice MacAulay, Bob and Sally Elliott, Rene Drumm, Ame Wiger, Meredith Guich, Mary Maxwell, Kaye Centers, Tara Broughten, Shannon Sharkey, Katherine Morris, Madelyn Swift, Gretchen Rode, Amy Elliott, Maryann Przybylski, Julie O'Keefe, Roxy Arneson, Martha Kouatli, Mary Cahill, Deb Kratz, Renee Torbenson, Laura Berger, Jennifer Clarke, Mary Paananen, Cindy Dalbec, Mary Ellen Frost, Anne Murray, Luann Baumann, Ilene Olson, Barb Bishop, Glen Palm, Eleanor Corner, Karin Winsher-Ihnen, and Rose Allen.

I thank Ada Alden, David Bredehoft, Deane Gradous, Russell Osnes, and Carol Kuechler.

Special thanks to Athalie Terry and Barbara Beystrom whose daily support helped make this book emerge.

Finally, thanks to all of the people who have taught me about Transactional Analysis. The importance of the "I'm OK, You're OK" way of interacting is the basis of this book.

Introduction: When Time-Out Isn't Working

Josh is off the wall today! He's had seven time-outs and he still isn't behaving. I'm at my wits'end.

Josh's mother's pain is obvious, and most parents can remember times when a child marched around the edge of their patience. This parent is not alone.

All children need to learn how to behave and when they misbehave they need some kind of discipline. Parents and care givers, with the welfare of the child in their hearts and a desire for a safe, peaceful atmosphere in their minds, look for methods of discipline that will stop the unwanted action and *also* build better behavior in the future.

The Latin root for the word discipline means "to teach." The goal of discipline is to teach children to have their own internal discipline based on their positive self-concept, not on fear or shame.

> Children need to learn to take care of their own behavior for themselves, not to please, placate, or be rewarded by others.

Time-Out is a logical discipline tool, and it is safer than spanking or criticizing. But when it does not have a calming effect or does not result in better behavior, parents and care givers need additional discipline tools. If Time-Out is not teaching what the child needs to learn, parents can use or add Time-In.

Time-In interrupts or avoids misbehavior when care givers use one of the four **A's: Ask, Act, Attend,** or **Amend.** I will explore these tools on later pages, as well as the differences between Time-Out and Time-In. If a child feels isolated or abandoned by Time-Out, Time-In puts the child back in contact with the parents. Time-In, used correctly, can strengthen the parent–child bond, build the child's trust in caring adults, and invite the child to feel cared about and supported. In addition, Time-In can prevent many problems because it is not a single tool. It is an overall approach that teaches the child *how to be competent, to think, and to succeed.*

The principle of connectedness behind Time-In works with children of all ages. However, parents of babies and toddlers will need to adapt use of two of the tools, **Ask** and **Amend,** to their child's level of development. As the child reaches age three, he or she will be able to answer questions and understand the concept of making amends more readily.

For parents who wish to be assertive without being authoritarian, who want to avoid being overly permissive, or who just want a new way to look at the parenting skills they already have, Time-In can be helpful.

1

What Is Time-In?

I spend quality time with Matt as often as I can. Isn't that Time-In?

Time-In is more than quality time, which is time spent directly attending to a child. Time-In is a four-part process that helps parents and teachers connect with children, teach them to solve their own problems, and become responsible for the outcomes of their actions and attitudes. Frequent use of Time-In can improve children's overall behavior.

The four parts of Time-In are:

These are discipline tools many adults are already using. Thinking of them as the four puzzle pieces of Time-In can help parents and care givers use them even more effectively. All children need to learn to listen when **Asked,** to assess and respond to **Actions,** to **Attend** to themselves and others, and to make **Amends** when needed.

The puzzle pieces can be used in any order. Sometimes all four are needed to resolve a behavior problem. Often, if parents stop to think about what lesson the child needs to learn, one or two pieces will do the job. Any of the four can help the child feel connected. All children need to belong and they behave better when they feel connected to the family or the classroom group. But connecting cannot be done in a minute. It takes time, time spent connecting with a child directly, in loving and structure-setting ways.[1]

But, you say, *I spend a lot of time with my children.* Time-In is different from *time-with;* although Time-In can occur during time-with. Children need lots of time with their parents and other adults. During time-with activities, children watch us, imitate us, and by informal social learning, capture many of the skills and lessons they need to manage and enjoy things in life and to live with others in society. We spend time with children when we play together, clean a drawer, read, sing, snuggle, do the laundry, bake cookies, and hundreds of other daily life activities.

However, simply doing time-with activities does not assure that the child will feel connected. In fact, the child may feel ignored, criticized, bored, or neglected. But time-with experiences can become a Time-In way of connecting. For example, time with a child watching television can become Time-In when the adult discusses with the child how a behavior they have just watched might hurt or help people if someone in their family did it. *Connection is built when adults share ideas with respect and encourage the child's ability to think.*

This connection is not built in a single grand event, but bit by bit, piece by piece, experience by experience. Time-In occurs only when the child feels heard, acknowledged, taken into account, and is affirmed for being capable. It takes a lot of loving experiences for a child to feel firmly connected with adults and to believe that they will stand by him while he makes mistakes and gradually learns how to behave. We strengthen connections every time we use one of the four Time-In puzzle pieces in a firm, loving way.

> Time-In is not one single discipline act: It is the process of attending, acting, asking, and amending over and over again.

Time-In is not only a set of tools to teach the lessons of discipline, the four **A's** themselves are important life lessons. Time-In is probably the most valuable way parents can use their time. As we explore Time-In you can decide when, how often, with which child, and for which problem any of the four puzzle pieces might be effective. You will also notice examples in which the discipline lesson is more for the parent than for the child. That is the nature of good parenting. We learn as we teach our children.

References

[1]Clarke, Jean Illsley, and Connie Dawson. *Growing Up Again: Parenting Ourselves, Parenting Our Children.* 2nd edition. Center City, Minn.: Hazelden, 1998. Has helpful explanations and examples of structure, the firm boundaries that let children feel secure.

2

Why Is Time-In Like a Puzzle with Four Pieces?

I find a discipline method that works with Bryan and I think I have discipline solved. But a few months later it doesn't work anymore and Bryan is up to his old tricks, with some new ones added. Will I ever solve this puzzle of discipline?

Time-In is called a puzzle with four pieces because finding a response to misbehavior that works is like a puzzle. When adults do find a method of discipline that stops unwanted behavior and lessens the chances of that behavior occurring in the future, often that discipline tool does not work later with—

- a different kind of problem,
- a different child,
- the same child at a different age,
- or just on a different day.

Parents, teachers, and caregivers who use the puzzle pieces of Time-In—**Ask, Act, Attend,** and **Amend**—can alter their discipline approaches by starting with any of the four pieces, using just one, or putting them together in any order. The **Attend** piece is always in the adult's awareness and helps the adult choose which piece to use directly with the child, and whether that piece is helping the child learn the lesson he needs.

Andrew threw a ball in the child care center. Teacher decided Andrew needed to learn to remember the rule about the ball. She did not glare at him, but got on his eye level and asked firmly, "Andrew, what is the rule about the ball?" Andrew started to protest and then said, "Oh, I forgot we aren't supposed to throw the ball inside. Only roll it." He picked the ball up and rolled it toward a playmate.

This time the teacher and Andrew solved the discipline puzzle with only one piece.

Discipline does not always work that easily.

The children were eating an after-school snack. Mom heard the crash, turned, and asked, "What happened?" Each child blamed the other. **Ask** *was not working. Mom decided the lesson to be taught was that it costs money to replace broken things, so she would teach that by getting the children to* **Attend** *to the broken pitcher. "Okay, help me sweep up this broken glass. I'm going to the shopping center in an hour. You both know how to read price tags. Bring a paper and pencil and make notes on the prices of pitchers like this one. Then we'll choose one and each make suggestions about how to pay for it."* (If the children pay for the pitcher, that would add an **Amend** piece.)

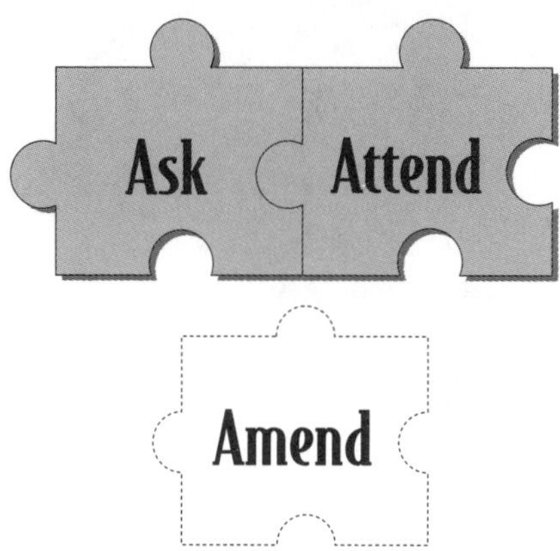

In both of these examples the children were invited to think and to learn. Sometimes the adults also need to learn new lessons, more effective ways to act. Consider all the different ways the puzzle pieces could be combined. I will include examples throughout the book.

3

How Does Time-In Differ from Time-Out and Other Common Methods of Discipline?

Okay, young lady! When we get home you are going to have a Time-Out!

The idea of Time-Out was welcomed by many parents who wanted an option to physical punishment and sarcasm.

Spanking, ridiculing, and shaming stop an unwanted behavior at the moment, but children respond to them for external reasons: fear of physical hurt and fear of psychological hurt. Those methods may stimulate the child to think about how to avoid the punishment, but they do not ask him to think about why the behavior was annoying or hurtful. When spanking, criticizing, and shaming are used, the adult has already done the thinking and the child's job is to respond to their thinking. The motivation to change behavior is external. The child may learn to think with these techniques, but often will not.

Time-Out, asking a child to calm himself and think, is a step toward internal motivation, the foundation for lasting behavior change to benefit the child and the family or group.

Time-Out was originally designed to provide cool-down time and space for a child who was upset. The child might be held and soothed or put in a certain spot to quiet herself, whichever worked best for that child. After she was calm she could think about what to do differently. Or she could be ready to take in the discipline (teaching) that was to follow.

Time-Out as Connection

Time-Out, as it was first described, built the connection between adult and child. It was not intended as a negative consequence, but as a gift of time and space to help the child, a positive interruption of behavior or over-excitement, a time to pull back, and a chance to start over, as in a sports event[1, 2, 3] Time-Out has several advantages:

- It can be an easy, instant way to interrupt and stop unwanted behavior.
- The introverted child may be able to think better during some time alone.
- The child who has something interesting in her room may welcome a little time to do a favorite activity and therefore become more calm.
- The child may become more calm if he has been taught how to calm himself or if an adult goes to a quiet place with him to rub his back.
- If the child knows why she is given Time-Out and she has a secure parent–child bond, she may use some solitary time to remember how to act appropriately.
- The parent may want space away from the child to help the parent calm down.

Time-Out Doesn't Always Work

Even though Time-Out can be a powerful tool, if it is used for every misbehavior it will miss the mark and become punishment. Punishment is hurting children, inflicting physical or psychological pain. Discipline is teaching. Children misbehave for many reasons (see chapter 9) and Time-Out may not offer the lessons needed for some of them. Also, when we isolate a child for Time-Out and forget or neglect to follow up with appropriate discipline that teaches a needed lesson, there are sound reasons why we may not be getting the results we want. Here are some of them:

- A child who is naturally extroverted may need to talk in order to think. He sorts out his thoughts as he babbles. Time-Out alone shuts down his thinking.[2]
- Children whose personality style is to process experiences with feelings first and thinking later may experience Time-Out alone as shutting down feelings and shutting off thinking.
- If the child lacks information or skills, Time-Out by herself does not provide them, and she may feel abandoned.
- Calm physical touching and holding usually reassures a child who is upset. Time-Out by himself may seem to be a withdrawal of love—a very frightening thing for a child.

- Children may view Time-Out as rejection of their noise, crying, or raging. Making noise is natural for children, and crying and raging are ways that children release tension and let us know that they are sad or frustrated.
- Time-Out may lose its effectiveness as the child grows older.

Time-Out as Punishment

"Bad children don't go to Time-Out; upset children do," says Madelyn Swift in *Discipline For Life!*[3] But it has become a common practice to use Time-Out as punishment for "bad children" and to isolate them when they have misbehaved.

When children regard Time-Out as punishment, they often use their discomfort to fuel blame and anger at the parent. They may use Time-Out to figure out how to get even rather than using the time to calm themselves and think about how to improve their behavior. When Time-Out is held over a child's head as a threat, it is apt to encourage the child to disconnect. The child may decide he has to behave in a certain way to avoid an outside punishment, and so does not need to behave when the adult is not around, rather than learning to behave well from internal motivation.

How Time-In Is Different

Time-Out and Time-In have the same goals: to interrupt or prevent misbehavior and to avoid misbehavior in the future. Unlike Time-Out, Time-In is not a single discipline tool. It has four ways to go about solving the puzzle of discipline.

These four can be combined in many ways, and Time-Out can be used as part of any of them. Used thoughtfully, they strengthen the bond between adult and child while they encourage the child to avoid or correct misbehavior for three internal reasons:

- He is developing a self-image of himself as a responsible, successful person.
- She understands that the rules are for her welfare and the welfare of the family or group.
- He feels that he is a contributing, valued member of the family or classroom.

Positive discipline allows a child to tap into his normal, healthy urge to learn to get along with his group. In *The Healing Connection* Jean Baker Miller reminds us that ". . . the goal of development is . . . the ability to participate actively in relationships that foster the well-being of everyone involved."[4]

Ways to use each of the four puzzle pieces are offered in the following chapters. You can think about how you might use Time-Out as part of each piece.

References

[1]Nelsen, Jane and H. Stephen Glenn. *Time-Out: Abuses and Effective Uses.* Fair Oaks, Calif.: Sunrise Press, 1992. Spells out how to use Time-Out.

[2]Kurcinka, Mary Sheedy. *Raising Your Spirited Child.* New York: HarperCollins, 1991, 1998. Helpful information on personality types and on living with children who run on fast-forward. Also by Mary Sheedy Kurcinka, *Raising Your Spirited Child Workbook.* New York, HarperCollins, 1998.

[3]Swift, Madelyn. *Discipline For Life! Getting It Right With Children.* Fort Worth, Tex.: Stairway Education Programs, 1998. Has a helpful description of Time-Out and other discipline methods.

[4]Miller, Jean Baker, M.D. and Irene Pierce Stiver, Ph.D. *The Healing Connection: How Women Form Relationships in Therapy and in Life.* Boston: Beacon Press, 1997.

4

Why

Michael snatched a car from Amy. In a firm, clear voice Dad asked, "Michael, what is the rule about toys?" Michael handed the car back and said, "Take turns."

Why ask, you ask? Because asking invites a child to think. When you tell the child, you have already done the thinking. Ask because asking teaches a child to listen. Children can turn off their ears to telling. Ask because you get more information when you ask than when you tell. Ask because true asking, not criticism hiding as asking, helps you connect with your child.

What to Ask

To use the **Ask** puzzle piece for discipline, first ask yourself, *What lesson does this child need to learn?*

Then ask yourself, *Is there a question that will help this child discover for herself what she needs to learn?*

If the answer to the second question is yes, frame the question and ask it. (If the answer is no, move to **Act, Attend,** or **Amend.**)

Ask questions about behavior. *Exactly what happened here?* is more apt to get helpful information than, *Why did you do that?* Avoid asking, *Why did you do that?* unless you think the misbehavior was caused by a lack of information. Usually children do not want to admit why or they may not even know why. Never say, *What made you do that?* because that tells the child some outside influence, not she, herself, is responsible for her behavior.

> Avoid putting "Okay?" at the end of a question or a directive, unless you are offering a genuine choice.

It's time to get your coat on, okay? or *I want you to pick up your toys, okay?* suggests that the child has a choice or should be agreeable or is in charge of the situation. If you mean, *Do you understand?* ask that.

When you ask, *Who tracked mud on the floor?* and the child knows you know he did it, you create distance and suspicion. The child either thinks you are stupid for asking or else goes on the defensive because the question sounds like a trick. Do not ask about what you already know.

Ask only questions the child can answer. Avoid asking questions that are too complex for the child's age. Ask only as many questions as are needed. *Do you remember the rule? Why do you think we have that rule? What do you think would happen if nobody in our family followed that rule? Why is it important for you to follow that rule?*

How and When to Offer Discipline by Asking

We ask questions of children all of the time. We ask what they want; we ask how they are feeling; we ask about their activities and achievements; we ask where they are going and what they are going to do. We ask them to be with us and to do things for us and do they know that we love them. And we ask for a gazillion other reasons.

But when we use the **Ask** puzzle piece as a way of disciplining children, we are asking in order to teach a lesson. Here is a beginning list of ideas about asking. As you read the ideas and the examples, you will probably think of other ideas that fit in your family or your classroom. Although the examples may not fit exactly for your child, you can use them to trigger your thinking about what will work in your situation.

When the child has misbehaved, choose the question to teach the needed lesson.

Jerrod, eight, left his bicycle in the driveway one more time. Dad could start with questions like these: *Jerrod, what would happen if a delivery truck ran over your bike? . . . How would you get to your friends' houses? I would not drive you, that is what your bike is for. . . How would you get the money for a new bike? . . . Is this what you want to have happen? . . .* The discipline lesson: put your bike away.

Ask in a clear, firm but not critical tone.

Anna, seven, left her coat on the floor for the umpteenth time. Mother sat down, calmed herself, and in a clear, firm, pleasant voice asked, *Anna, do you know where Daddy's coat belongs? . . . Right, in the closet. Where does Luke's coat belong? . . . Right, on the peg.* Mom grinned and asked, *Can you guess what question I'm going to ask next?* Anna grinned back and hung up her coat.

Mom gave her a big hug. The discipline lesson: hang up your coat.

Ask to help the child start choosing from options.

Tommy, three, needs to wear his shoes. *Tommy, we are going to the store very soon and we are all going to wear shoes. Do you want to put your shoes on or shall I put them on you?* If Tommy does not put on his shoes, Mother uses the **Act** puzzle piece. She says, *I see you chose to have me put your shoes on you,* and she does so, even if Tommy squalls. Discipline lesson: Decide among options of how to comply.

Obedience is important, but in a democracy it is not enough. Citizens need to be able to think, and asking questions encourages thinking. We start asking as discipline about age two. Before that we have asked to teach vocabulary, *Where is your nose?* and to get information, *Do you want some milk?* Age two is a good time to start teaching children to think about options. Also, giving a child a choice of two or three options, all of which are agreeable to you, helps to reduce hassles.

Ask to encourage thinking and responsibility.

Zach, five, had been scolded by Grandma for riding his tricycle beyond where she could see him. Zach fussed at his mother about having been scolded. *Grandma was mean to me.* Mother asked, *You have to listen to Grandma even if you think she's mean. Do you think Grandma could have been scared?*

No, she was mad.

If she had been scared, what would she have been scared about?

I don't know.

It's Grandma's job to protect you. Can she do that if she can't see you?

I guess not.

So, where are you supposed to ride your tricycle?

Where she can see me.

Yes! You got that! (High five)

If Zach had not responded positively, Mother could have moved to **Act** and removed the tricycle for a day. Discipline lesson: Learn about following rules even if you don't like the way you are reprimanded.

Get the child's attention before you ask.

Leticia, two, had a tantrum in the grocery store. Dad parked his grocery cart, carried Leticia to the car, and waited calmly until she finished storming. Then, looking straight at her, he asked, *Are you ready to use your indoor voice now?* She nodded yes. *We are going to finish shopping now. Will you remember to use your indoor voice to tell me what you want?* She nodded yes. Discipline lesson: No tantrums in public places.

Ask to remind children of a rule that is not negotiable.

Terri, six, smacked her little brother because he took her baby doll. Lisa, the baby-sitter, made sure the boy was okay and then took Terri aside. Lisa asked, *Terri, what is the rule in your family about hitting?*

Dunno.

Shall we go look at the rule chart on the kitchen door?

It's no hitting.

So what are you supposed to do instead?

But he took my baby doll!

So what are you supposed to do instead?

Use words?

Yes, Terri, use your words.

But I did.

So, then?

I'm supposed to ask you for help.

So ask.

Okay, will you help me?

Lisa ruffled Terri's hair and they went off to retrieve the toy. Lisa's action of ruffling Terri's hair reestablished connection and invited Terri to change to a positive emotional state. Young children need to be told the rules many times before they remember. Discipline lesson: Solve problems without hitting.

Make sure that the child hears and responds to the question.

Chelsey, four, is wearing the necklace that Amanda had reported missing from her cubby. Teacher takes Chelsey aside and asks, *Chelsey, when someone takes something of yours without asking, what are they supposed to do?*

I didn't take anything.

Chelsey, you didn't answer my question. What are they supposed to do?

I don't know.

Shall we ask the other teacher?

No.

Can you remember now?

Give it back?

Yes! Do you want me to help you give back the necklace?

No, I'll put it back.

Discipline lesson: Don't take others' belongings without asking.

Ask children to help figure out negotiable rules.

The Millers have a nonnegotiable rule that Chris, seven, may watch no more than six hours of television a week and Ben, ten, may watch seven. The Millers know that children need some rules that are negotiable in order for children to learn how to think and to negotiate. So the rule about *what* they watch is negotiable. They may watch separately or together, but they must decide what they will watch and a parent must approve their choices. Mother asks, *Ben and Chris, do you want to choose your television programs for the week and bring them to me or do you want me to help you choose?*

Can we have more hours this week because the Olympics are on and we need to watch skiing?

I don't think so, but choose your programs and tell me good reasons you should get to watch them.

Okay.

Chris, if you need help choosing, how will you get that?

I'll ask Ben.

Discipline lesson: How to negotiate with family members.

Ask to help a child through shame.

Todd, ten, has been looking downcast and avoiding his parents for two days. Mother asks, *Todd, I see something is bothering you. We need you to talk with your dad or me. Which will it be?*

I don't want to talk.

I see that. But, when something is bothering us, we need to get support from our family. So when do you think you'll be ready for that?

There's nothing you can do.

Perhaps, but we can be on your team. You know we will love you no matter what. Wouldn't you be surprised if we really could help?

Yah, big time!

So, I'll ask you again tomorrow.

If Todd still says no, parents may switch to **Act** and find a trusted adult Todd will talk with. Discipline lesson: If you have done something you are ashamed of, it is better to get your parents' support.

Ask to remind about natural consequences.

Steve, twelve, has had a very short fuse lately and last night he had a temper tantrum. In a serious, uncritical voice Dad asked, *Steve, when you blew up last night you reminded me of the temper tantrums you had when you were two. Did it feel like that to you?*

I guess so.

Does that seem like an okay way for a guy your age to show his anger?

I guess not, but I couldn't help it.

You've said you want a job at McDonald's some day. What do you think would happen if you blew up there?

I'd be fired?

Could be. Will you think about other ways to handle anger and whether allowing yourself to have a big blow-up is worth the price you may have to pay for it?

Discipline lesson: Unrestrained displays of temper at age twelve can be costly.

Ask to reinforce positive behavior.

Toddler Addie is carrying two books and drops one. Mom asks, *Addie, will you bring the book that is on the floor so I can read to you?* Addie brings the book. Mom hugs her and says, *You know how to pick up books!*

Parents want children to learn to follow directions and to expect to get attention for good behavior.

Adam, nine, usually has to be reminded to clear his dishes after a meal. This night he does so without being asked. Dad asks, *Son, do you know why I like it when you clear your dishes without my telling you?*

No, I don't.
I'd rather play catch with you than nag you! Get your glove.

> When you **Ask,** do not ask to criticize and do not ask a question that sounds like a trap. **Ask** the question that teaches the lesson the child needs to learn.

How Do You Act?

Angela knew the toy plane was an outdoor toy. When she hurled it across the living room, Mother quickly picked up the plane and placed it on the high "'Til Tomorrow" shelf. Angela begged to have it back. Mother shook her head no and went on with what she was doing.

You act decisively because there is a situation that calls for action. You act, move your body, to interrupt or prevent a misbehavior and to teach a needed lesson. To take physical action is often the best way to connect with and get the attention of misbehaving children. The issue may be safety or protection of property, or it may be a situation of psychological threat. It may be time to act because talking or asking about a misbehavior has not worked. Or you act to teach a child who ignores what is going on around her to pay attention.

When to Act and What to Act Upon

You can use the **Act** puzzle piece in any situation where you think your action will be more effective than **Asking** or **Attending** or **Amending.**

Sometimes your action will redirect behavior, sometimes your action will enforce a logical consequence for misbehavior, and sometimes your action will be to stand by and allow the natural consequences to teach the lesson.

Always start to move if your own sense of urgency says, "Somebody better do something right now, pronto!"

Always act if you think **Asking, Attending,** or **Amending** won't help the situation. **Act** is the puzzle piece that is most likely to be effective with toddlers who are not yet ready for asking or attending or amending.

Sometimes you have to act to rescue a kid or calm him down with Time-Out before you can teach the needed lesson with **Asking** or **Amending.**

Sometimes you can act before there is an outbreak of whining or fighting.

How and When to Offer Discipline by Acting

We act, we do things with children on a daily basis. We eat with them, teach them how to do things, and play with them. We go places with them and do chores with them. We do dozens of things with children.

When we use the **Act** puzzle piece as a method of discipline, our action is intended to teach a specific lesson. Here are examples of ways some adults have acted successfully. As you read you will recognize that some of these might not be successful with your child, but you can think of other actions you could take and other situations you would act upon. Spanking is acting, but it is a punishment. Think about ways of acting that challenge the child to think and be responsible.

Act to prevent an accident or problem.

When toddler Jimmy headed for the cut-glass bowl, Grandma quickly placed it out of his reach and gave him some plastic bowls to play with. Problem prevented: Breaking a bowl.

When Bailey, two, picked up a sharp knife to help make a sandwich, Grandpa said, *Danger, Bailey. Sharp, sharp. Use this one* and handed her a butter knife. Injury prevented: Cut hand.

When Teacher learned that watching television, any television, even educational television, slows the growth of the brains of young children,[1] she turned off the television in her child care center and gave the children other things to do. Learning problem prevented: Reluctance to try or to persevere.

When Dad heard that some eleven-year-olds in Lanesha's class were drinking alcohol, he put a lock on the liquor cabinet and explained to Lanesha it was to make sure no playmates tried to drink at her house and to remind her there is a reason for a legal age for drinking. Discipline problem prevented: Children drinking alcohol.

Act to reinforce a rule or an expected behavior.
Kyle, two, who had been bathed, read to, and put to bed, padded out demanding a story. The baby-sitter very matter-of-factly walked him back, put him in bed, and said, *Good night, Kyle.* She did this as many times as Kyle got up. Discipline lesson: Bedtime means stay in bed.

Act to get a child's attention when other methods of discipline have not been effective.
Ian, age twelve, was increasingly rude and sarcastic despite frequent reminders and asking. During dinner he put down his sisters and made gross complaints about the food. Dad decided to see if a surprise action would get Ian's attention. Dad stood up suddenly and put Ian's food in the refrigerator. As he returned to his own dinner he said, *Ian, I know that it is common for junior high kids to complain and to put each other down, but we expect you to remember not to do that at home. You may finish eating after you have spoken civilly to each one of us.* Discipline lesson: Live up to family standards and values.

Act to redirect an activity or to interrupt misbehavior.
Toddler Rachael reached for a figurine on Grandma's shelf. Mom clapped her hands, picked up Rachael, and said, *Let's show Grandma how we dance.*

Dad noticed that the nine- to twelve-year-olds playing basketball were not challenging the player who was cheating. Suddenly Dad was part of the game, dribbling, shooting baskets, and passing. Just as suddenly he stood still, held the ball to his chest, and said, *In this yard everyone plays by the rules.* He tossed the ball to the one who had been cheating, grinned, and left. Dad directed attention to the cheating without a lecture or shaming. Discipline lesson: Play by the rules.

Act to let consequences teach.

When reminded to do his chores, Nick, eight, growled, *I won't and you can't make me*. Dad looked at him squarely and said, *You are a member of this family and everyone is expected to do their share. You are right, I can't make you do your chores, but it is a parent's job to be sure kids are mighty uncomfortable if they don't do their share.*

Dad took a pad of paper and said, *Help me make a list of ways you might be uncomfortable if you don't do your chores.* Nick glowered at his dad and moved off to do his chores. Discipline lesson: Everyone contributes to the family welfare.

The rule at Sophie's house is to use a big girl voice when asking for things. Sophie, three, whined for cookies. Mother said matter-of-factly, *Cookies are for girls who ask with their big girl voice,* as she picked up the cookie jar and placed it on a high shelf. Discipline lesson: Whining does not get you what you want.

> Parents have to be able to allow children to experience uncomfortable consequences of misbehavior.

Act to help a child deal with feelings.

Kaitlin, seventeen months, had a delightful day at child care, did not want to leave, and had her first flat-out-kicking-and-screaming tantrum when she got home. Mom sat on the floor beside her and repeated in a gentle voice, *You are okay. You will get through this. You are okay.* Kaitlin finished her tantrum and was pleasant all evening. Discipline lesson: All of your feelings are okay.

Derek, two and a half, had pillows in a safe corner that he could pound and kick when he needed to. If he had a tantrum and hit and kicked other children, Teacher immediately guided him to the corner saying, *Let me know when you are through. Then we will talk about what you can do instead of hitting.* Discipline lesson: All of your feelings are okay and you are not to hurt others.

Ever since Ashley, eleven, found out the family was going to move, she had been grumpy and uncooperative at home and at school. Her teacher included a geography lesson on the city Ashley was moving to and helped the children plan a going away party. Ashley's mom got the *Help for Kids! Understanding Your Feelings About Moving*[2] book and did the saying good-bye and saying hello activities in it with Ashley. Discipline lesson: Get help with a problem instead of being grumpy.

Act to teach delayed gratification.

Being able to delay gratification is an important life skill and is best taught from an early age by carrying through on when/then directions. Mitchell, seven, wanted to go out and play before his chores were done. Mom handed him a basket of clean clothes and said, *When you have finished your chores and put your clothes away, then you can go out and play.* Discipline lesson: Delayed gratification.

Mike, four, wanted the play dough. Teacher took the play dough off the shelf and held it up. *When you have put your ball in the basket and sat down at the table, then you may play with the play dough.* Discipline lesson: Delayed gratification.

Justin, eleven, wanted a radio-controlled airplane. Dad took Justin to the store to look at planes and said, *I'll help you choose one that won't break easily and when you have saved half of the cost we'll get one.* Discipline lesson: Delayed gratification.

Act to interrupt sibling squabbling.

The siblings, seven and ten, were squabbling. Mom asked them to stop, but they did not respond. Mom placed her body squarely between them and said firmly, *Kids, you need to listen to me! I have placed two chairs across the room from each other. Each of you sit on a chair and take a Time-Out to simmer down so you can think. As soon as you think of one way you can solve your problem move your chair forward a bit. When you think of a second way, move it some more. A third, still more. When your chairs get near, tell each other your ideas, choose the one that will work, and come and tell me about it. I'll be watching, but not listening.* Discipline lesson: Use your thinking skills instead of fighting.

Act to stop tattling.

Carmen, eight, and Maya, five, had been tattling on each other. Mother showed them a poster on which she had printed

Telling or Tattling?	
Children tattle when they want to— • get someone in trouble, • look good in someone else's eyes, • get attention, • have an adult solve their problem.	**Children are telling when they—** • want protection for themselves or some-one else, • want protection for their own or someone else's property, • are scared, • are in danger, • want help in solving their problem.

From *Telling Isn't Tattling* by K. Hammerseng. Used with permission.

She said, *You girls have been tattling on each other and it's time to learn the difference between tattling and telling. Run and get your teddy bears and we'll teach them, too.* Mother made up little stories about the bears that were clearly either tattling or telling. After each story she asked if that was tattling or telling and checked out the answer against the poster. When the girls continued to tattle, she read the book *Telling Isn't Tattling*[3] with them, and they talked about each example. Discipline lesson: Solve your problems yourself unless there is danger to a person or property.

Act to reinforce and clarify positive behavior.

Some children blow off verbal praise but will take in actions that reinforce success and positive behavior. Celeste, three, loved to have her mother play with her. When she followed a rule well, Mom said, *Hey! I want to play with a girl who remembers to put her books on the shelf. What shall we play?* Discipline lesson: There are positive responses to good behavior.

Jenny, eight, who loved to draw with her dad, had been struggling with her homework. When she finished it Dad handed her a big pad and felt pens and asked if she would help him draw a picture of her school and a proud girl carrying her homework to school. He thought about taking her out for ice cream, but decided to help her get internal gratification instead. Discipline lesson: Finishing a task can give internal satisfaction.

> **Act** to interrupt, redirect, help, or give a consequence, not to shame, ridicule, show up, or compete.

References

[1]DeGaetano, Gloria, M.Ed. *Television and the Lives of Our Children, Screen Smarts: A Family Guide to Media Literacy.* Redmond, Wash.: Train Of Thought Publishers, 1993. *Media Smarts 4 Young Folks.* Los Angeles, Calif.: Merrie Way Community, 1997.

[2]Gesme, Carole and Larry Peterson. *Help for Kids! Understanding Your Feelings About Moving.* Minneapolis, Minn.: Pine Press, 1991.

[3]Hammerseng, Kathryn M. *Telling Isn't Tattling.* Seattle, Wash.: Parenting Press, Inc., 1995. This is a helpful book to use with children.

6

What Does Attend Mean?

When Jacob, six, pushed Paul into a locker and scraped Paul's elbow, Teacher insisted Jacob attend to Paul. After Jacob picked up Paul's books and found a bandage, Teacher asked Jacob to attend to himself by thinking about the question, "What do I need so I can be with other kids without hurting them?"

To attend means to pay close attention to what is happening in the here and now. It means carefully assessing the situation and making a judgment about what to do. For a parent, it means paying attention to what is needed in the immediate situation and in the larger picture of teaching children about values and responsibility. Often it presents a new learning, a discipline lesson, for parents. For children past the baby stage it means learning to attend to the results of their misbehavior. It also means learning to attend to their own needs and learning skills that avoid misbehavior.

What to Attend to

The **Attend** puzzle piece can help you focus on many aspects of a behavior problem. In one sense the **Attend** piece always floats above or hovers over the other three.

> Only by **Attending** will you choose the appropriate puzzle piece: **Ask** the helpful question, take the right **Action,** or notice the misbehavior that needs to be **Amended.**

Attending will help you choose the lesson you want your child to learn. Then you move to **Ask, Act,** or **Amend.** Sometimes you **Act** to teach your child how to attend to a broken object or a hurt playmate. Other times you **Ask** your child to attend to his own needs. You may insist that the child **Attend** to your level of distress about what he has done by making **Amends.**

Sometimes you **Attend** to the environment to help avoid further problems. You **Attend** regularly to the needs of infants and young children while gradually teaching them to **Attend** to the needs of others. Sometimes you **Attend** to your own level of frustration or your anger as a signal that you need to look beyond this particular discipline incident. You may need new skills, more support, or some outside help with a particular child. You may need to look for causes behind the misbehavior (see chapter 9).

How and When to Use the Attending Puzzle Piece

All parents and teachers attend to misbehavior in one way or another, especially to behavior problems that do not get resolved by what usually works. Here are some ways that adults have used the **Attend** puzzle piece to address those problems and ways they have taught children to attend. You can probably add dozens of others. Notice that many of the solutions involve more doing than talking because children often learn better by doing than by listening. Most of the discipline lessons are for children, but some turned out to be for the adults.

Attend to a broken object or a hurt child.

One way to avoid giving lots of attention to a misbehaving child is to focus on the results of the misbehavior. This may cut down on the child's desire to misbehave and also teach some empathy.

When Will, three, smashed a toy, Teacher asked Will to attend to the broken toy. *Will, this toy is broken. You can't play with it unless we can fix it. Do you think we can do that? How?* Discipline lesson: Breaking a rule may lose you a privilege.

If a child has been hurt, the teacher can attend to the hurt child in a way that does not give the misbehaving child lots of attention.

In the preschool room, Rebecca, four, had thrown a toy and hurt Amy. Teacher moved in immediately and got Rebecca's attention. *Rebecca, Amy has been hurt. You stay beside us while I help Amy.* Teacher applied first aid, not looking at Rebecca, but making sure Rebecca stayed put.

Then Teacher empowered Amy.

Amy, do you remember the rule about throwing toys?
Yes.
Amy, can you tell Rebecca that rule by yourself or shall I tell her for you?
Don't throw toys!
Amy, do you want to tell Rebecca how you feel?
I'm mad at you.

Teacher might ask Rebecca to make **Amends** or he might **Act** by sending Rebecca to the Time-Out thinking chair to think about what to do next time. Discipline lesson: Breaking a rule is a poor way to get attention.

Attend to rules that are consistently broken.

When rules are consistently broken, the attending adults look for underlying reasons.

Dad had a nagging feeling that the children, six, nine, and ten, were breaking more rules more often. He called the children to him and said, *Pay attention!* [**Attend**] *I need your thinking about a problem. You are breaking so many rules so often that it seems as if I'm always yelling at you. What's going on?* [**Ask**] The children told him that there were too many rules to remember, that the rules changed, and that he did not follow the rules! Together they chose the six most important rules and made a poster of them. [**Act**] Brandon, ten, made a wallet-sized copy for his dad to carry. The children decided that if their dad broke a rule they would stand in a row and all fuss at him. Dad said if the kids kept the rules they would all find a way to celebrate. Discipline lesson for parents: Rules must be reasonable, known, understood, and applicable to all in the family.

Attend to a child's needs and developmental level.

Sometimes discipline problems arise because we are expecting too much of children. The Wongs were concerned about how to get their daughter to do her chores independently. When the Wongs saw a chart[1] with the ages at which children actually do chores, they were surprised. They were expecting their little girl to do chores alone and without reminding that most other children her age still needed help with. The Wongs asked other parents what they expected, and posted some charts[2] with developmental information on the refrigerator to remind them to keep their expectations appropriate for their child's stage of development. Discipline lesson for adults: Choose chores suitable for a child's age.

Attend to children who are overly demanding.

All children need to learn that they are not the center of the universe. One way parents help children learn this hard lesson is by teaching them to wait. Mom and her friend were chatting. When toddler Kendall's Cheerios were gone she used her demanding *Uh!* to get her mother's attention. Mom said, *Your Cheerios are all gone. I'll get you some more, okay?* and moved to the kitchen. Kendall screamed. Mom attended to her own behavior. She started saying, *Wait,* instead of asking, *Okay?* This told Kendall what to do instead of asking for her agreement. Gradually Kendall learned to wait. Discipline lesson for adults: Tell young children what they need to do instead of asking their permission.

Attend to children's temperament.

Discipline that works with one child may not be helpful to a child with different temperament traits. When the family attended their house of worship, Sarah, six, wiggled and twisted and bumped her way through the service. Since trying to calm her down before the service hadn't worked, her parents made a way for her to exercise vigorously right before the service. Her job was to get all the wiggles and twists and bumps out ahead of time. Discipline lesson: Children need to recognize and learn to manage their own bodies and temperaments.[3]

Attend to children's social skills.

It takes years to develop good social skills, and children do a lot of experimenting along the way. Dan, five, bossed people around a lot. Mother was concerned about his social skills and she was afraid that Dan might be bullying other children. She encouraged him to slow down, step back, and sometimes do what other kids wanted to do. Dan gave her a puzzled look. Mother decided to get more information, so she consulted Dan's preschool teacher [**Attend**]. His teacher explained that she had observed Dan carefully and that he was a leader with followers who were willing to go along with Dan's demands because they had more fun and excitement than on the days when Dan was absent. She said children follow bullies out of fear and that Dan's influence was different.[4] Mother decided to get off Dan's case, but to help him smooth some of his rough edges [**Act**]. Discipline lesson for adults: Very young leaders who have been mistaken for bullies need to learn social skills.

Attend to the attitude behind disruptive behavior.
Although teaching social skills is essential, attending to the attitude behind children's disruptive behavior can be equally important. David, nine, got in frequent fights. Scoldings, groundings, loss of privileges did not make a difference. Dad decided to focus on David instead of on the fights [**Attend**]. He noticed that David seemed to think that he should fight about anything that he perceived as a threat, and he could see threats everywhere. During the following weeks, Dad and David took walks and played miniature golf together [**Act**]. First Dad helped David sort out real threats from shadow threats. Next they talked about fight and flee, and that real men know when to flee—to scram, to get the heck out of there. Then Dad taught David about fix or flow—all the times that neither fight nor flee is the best thing to do and he would have to find ways to solve a problem or move around it.

David did not think it would be easy to fix or flow when he really wanted to get out of the scene or pop somebody. Dad reminded David that fight and flee are responses that come from deep within the human experience. Long ago, when a young boy met a wild animal on the path, he needed to know instantly whether to flee or fight. Grab a stick and club the snake, or get away from the tiger.

David, however, meets different kinds of tigers in his everyday life. Sometimes they are physical, but usually they are social or psychological. David's dad explained that the fix and flow responses come from a different part of the brain, the cortex, which comes into play slightly after the primitive fight or flee response has been activated.

Dad recommended that on their walks they think of possible problems and then decide what the four responses, fight, flee, fix, or flow might be. Then, when a similar problem came up, David would have four options, not two, for solving it.

David recalled that last year at school, Brian, the leader of a group of boys, spread a rumor about Cody, one of the boys. Cody could not prove the rumor was not true because it was Brian's word against Cody's and many kids believed Brian. David would have wanted to split Brian's lip, but Cody had just held his head high as he walked by Brian and ignored him.

David and Dad thought about the four options Cody had:

1. Fight. Cody could have duked it out with Brian. If Brian had won, or had not apologized, that would not have settled the issue.
2. Flee. Cody could have stayed home from school or maybe even switched to another school. Staying home from school would not help Cody. Switching schools might.
3. Fix. Cody might have tried to fix the situation by telling the other kids what was true, but that would still be one person's word against another's. He might have spread rumors about Brian, which would increase the level of the conflict. He could have gone to the counselor or principal for help, but in his school the staff expected kids to solve their own problems.
4. Flow. Cody had decided to flow—to slide past the problem without giving Brian the satisfaction of acting upset. In

this sense, flow had worked. Cody spent some miserable days, but he kept his head high and Brian eventually tired of the game and stopped fanning the rumors. By the end of the school year, Cody had made a new group of friends who treated him well. Cody knew how to flow, he had the courage and determination to follow the flow path, and in this case it was a good decision.

Sometimes Fix is a better course of action. When Teacher accused Ana of copying a particularly well-done essay, Ana wanted to argue about it. Instead, she brought in the copies of the early revisions she had worked and reworked. Teacher was impressed and encouraged Ana to continue writing. Ana was glad she still had the earlier versions and decided she would make it a habit to keep a folder of her work until the final paper was accepted. Fixing worked better than fighting for Ana. Discipline lesson: Fighting is not enough. You also have to know when to flee and how to fix and flow.

Attend to children's problem-solving skills.

It takes a long time to learn good fixing or problem-solving skills. Children learn in small steps and often need coaching. When Dylan, seven, and Carly, eleven, finally drove their parents to the edge with constant squabbling, their parents decided to stop responding to each wrangle with scoldings and long talks and deliberately teach the children problem-solving skills. First they looked at their own skills and each chose two which they taught with humor by demonstrating what happened when they did and did not use the skills. Then they read some interactive books[5] and picked up more ideas. They encouraged the children to bring problem-solving ideas home from school and evaluate them. Soon the children were demonstrating things that did and did not work. If the children squabbled, they were challenged to invent their own new problem-solving method. Discipline lesson for adults: Focus on the solution, not on the squabble.

Attend to what is going on in the family.

Sometimes children's misbehavior is their response to something in the family that is not working for them. This may be easily identified when the parents attend, or it may be very subtle. It is almost always unintentional and parents are often surprised and chagrined when they figure out what is happening. It is important for parents not to stay stuck in guilt or shame, but to recognize that it is part of life in a family to accept that what is not working well in the family sometimes is reflected in a child's misbehavior. It is the parents' job to attend to any problem and to improve the environment for the children as much as possible.

Mr. Amato suspected that his children's misbehavior was at least partially a response to the divorce. He found a support group for the children and one for himself. Discipline lesson: Get outside help for big family stresses.

The Blakeleys realized that their seventeen-year-old son's mismanagement of money was a reflection of their own. The whole family went into financial management counseling. Discipline lesson: Both children and parents can learn new skills.

The Finseths were disturbed by their children's habit of blaming others instead of taking responsibility for their behaviors. When the Finseths listened to themselves they realized they blamed other drivers, their bosses, the neighbors, and the postal carrier, to name a few. They did not *really* blame those folks; it was just a habit to talk that way. But the children did not know that. Discipline lesson for parents: Children make their own interpretations of what they hear and see in the family.

Attend to what is going on with the child that you do not know about.

When there is a behavior problem that persists, parents often get help by searching out what is going on in the child's life that they do not know about. Parents ask the child, the school, friends, activity coaches, group leaders, anyone they think might shed light on the problem. If that does not work, they try to find a counselor the child will work with. The misbehavior may not give a clue about the cause. Here are situations that some school-age children experience:

- Nicki comes home looking for a fight because she believes she is too dumb to do school work.
- Max comes home looking for a fight because he is being ridiculed by classmates.
- Kevin's grades are dropping because he is preoccupied with gang activity.
- Sue's grades are dropping because she is fearful about being bullied.
- Hannah's grades are dropping because there is so much noise in the classroom she cannot hear the teacher.

- Rob has become distant at home because he is using drugs.
- Zenia has closed down and acts depressed because she was raped.
- Lessa is weepy because her "best friend" snubs her.
- Brent is grouchy and surly because several small stressors have piled up on him.

Discipline lesson for adults: Children often respond to stressors outside the family with misbehavior. Parents and schools need to attend to what is going on and take *whatever* action is necessary to make the child's world safe.

Attend to your own anger, frustration, and needs.

Anger and frustration are clues that we adults need to change our behaviors. Celeste was tired of being super mom and angry at doing more of the housework than the rest of the family. Discipline lesson for adults: Teach children to do household tasks and expect all family members to contribute.

Rick was uncomfortable with his children's lack of appreciation and respect. After all, he had always made sure they were totally comfortable and happy and he had shielded them from negative consequences of their behaviors. Discipline lesson for parents: Part of growing up is learning to handle discomfort, and parents have to learn to tolerate their children's discomfort.

Attend to positive behavior.

One of the surest ways to avoid misbehavior is to attend to positive behavior. Children need recognition and if they do not get it in positive ways, they will get it in negative ways. Recognition and attention are essential to health and growth.

For a week Roger counted the interactions he had with his daughter Nellie. He noticed that he responded to misbehavior three times as often as he did to good behavior. As Roger turned that around, Nellie's behavior improved. Discipline lesson for parents: When adults attend to positive behavior, negative behavior decreases.

> Caring adults **Attend** to a child by being or becoming aware of what is going on in the child's real world. Adults also teach children to **Attend** to the people, objects, and situations that are affected by the child's behavior.

References

[1]Crary, Elizabeth. *Pick Up Your Socks . . . and other skills growing children need!* Seattle, Wash.: Parenting Press, Inc., 1990. The chart is on page 51.

[2]Clarke, Jean Illsley and Connie Dawson. *Growing Up Again: Parenting Ourselves, Parenting Our Children,* 2nd edition. Center City, Minn.: Hazelden, 1998. Has charts that list developmental information for each stage of growth.

[3]Nelville, Helen, R.N. and Diane Clark Johnson, C.F.L.E. *Temperament Tools: Working with Your Child's Inborn Traits.* Seattle, Wash.: Parenting Press, Inc., 1998. Shick, Lyndall, M.A. *Understanding Temperament: Strategies for Creating Family Harmony.* Seattle, Wash.: Parenting Press, Inc., 1998.

[4]Grevstad, Marilyn. *Everyone Does It This Way.* WE Newsletter, Vol. 17, No. 1, Issue 94, Daisy Press, 16535 9th Ave. N, Minneapolis, MN, 55447, Jan. 1998. See also Budd, Linda S., Ph.D. *Living with the Active Alert Child.* Seattle, Wash.: Parenting Press, Inc., 1993.

[5]Crary, Elizabeth. *Children's Problem Solving Books* Series, 2nd edition, Seattle, Wash.: Parenting Press, Inc., 1996. Six books help young children ages preschool through grade two find optional ways to handle problems. Beekman, Susan and Jeanne Holmes. *Battles, Hassles, Tantrums & Tears.* New York: Hearst Books, 1993. Focuses on problem solving.

7

When Is It Important to Make Amends?

When Carrie lost Isaac's book, Mother asked Carrie to find a way to make it up to Isaac, in a way that Carrie would be proud of, that was acceptable to Isaac, and that seemed appropriate to Mother. After some negotiation, Isaac was willing to take one of Carrie's books to replace his missing book.

Making amends means making payment or atoning for loss, injury, or insult. It is important for children to learn to make amends when their misbehavior has caused physical or psychological harm to family members or to others. Making amends helps the child rebuild the connection he has broken with the person he has wronged. It is also important for children to make amends because of what it does for the child. It is important to understand that:

- Punishment hurts a child and it does not correct the wrong.
- Discipline that teaches a child does not necessarily right a wrong.
- Making amends rights a wrong and helps the child become a better person.

A grandparent who was sharing her wisdom about the four puzzle pieces said, *I didn't teach my children to make amends. I wish I had, but I didn't know how. But then, my parents didn't teach me to make amends. I hope my grandchildren learn how.*

Ah, yes, we cannot teach what we do not know unless we invent it or stumble into it. I, too, was not taught to make amends. I stumbled into it with my children when I felt strongly for a person they had wronged. Then I noticed how much better they felt about themselves after making amends. But I did not have a good, solid way to help children make amends until I found *Restitution: Restructuring School Discipline* by Diane Chelsom Gossen.[1] This wonderfully helpful book is written for schools, but the ideas apply just as well at home. I urge you to read it.

> "The act of restitution is a healing act for the person who has done wrong and it has the potential to remedy the wrong for the victim."
> —D. C. Gossen

I wish I had had this framework when my children were younger, and I think it is important for us to use it no matter what our children's ages.

What to Make Amends for

It is not reasonable to expect amends for every misbehavior because teaching children to make amends takes time, patience, and persistence. It is important to use the **Amend** puzzle piece to make amends for serious misbehaviors because it rights a wrong. Also, if the child feels ashamed and wants to hide or blame others, making amends can move her past the shame so she can feel competent and worthy again. Making amends, in contrast to a punishment, is a powerful builder of self-discipline and true self-esteem.

The most important way to use the **Amend** puzzle piece is to make amends to your child when you have wronged her. This teaches her that mistakes do not make one bad, but they are something to correct. It also teaches that the parent or teacher practices being responsible and expects responsible behavior from everyone in the family or group.

What you invite a child to make amends for depends on what you decide is important and then only if you have the time, energy, and patience to carry through. You do not ask a child to make amends just as you are saying good-bye. The **Amend** puzzle piece is like the **Act** one, but very specific.

How and When to Make Amends

Amends are payments or atonement made for injury, insult, or loss. Depending on the situation, the amends might be made with money, time, services, objects repaired, or any other way that is agreeable to the person to whom the restitution is being made. Younger children may ask adults for suggestions. Older children need to figure out what to do on their own. When the amending person is young, the atonement must also be approved by a parent, teacher, or other involved adult to be sure it is appropriate. The age at which adult approval is no longer necessary will depend upon the maturity and good judgment of the child.

While adults sometimes make amends years after the offense takes place, it is better to have children make amends immediately or within a few days.

The adult guiding the process starts with *How can you fix this?* rather than with criticism or moralizing. The adults always monitor the process so that the amends chosen do not somehow reward the misbehavior and encourage further offense.

Adults also watch for signs that the amends are genuine. *I have a necklace at home that I don't like. I'll give Tanya that for the one I broke* would not be accepted by the adult. If amends are suggested by the person who was wronged, make sure they are about righting the wrong, not about getting even. If the wronged person refuses to let go of the hurt and accept the amends, stop the amending process and use **Act, Ask,** or **Attend** to deal with the perpetrator.

The following guidelines need not be addressed in a specific order, nor will every single point apply in a given situation. But they offer an overview of what is involved in helping children make amends. These examples about damaged property and a broken promise may not reflect misbehavior in your family, but you can think of ways to adapt each example to your situation.

Damaged Property

The child making amends must put forth effort. Teacher responds to a howl from the area by the easel where Noah, four, and Bobby, three, are glaring at each other. *Noah, when you tore Bobby's paper you ruined his artwork. What can you do to fix it?*

Noah looks at the floor and says, *I'm sorry.* Teacher puts a hand on Noah's shoulder and asks, *Okay, you are sorry. Now what can you do about it?*

Can you fix it?

This is your job. Can you think of something you can do?

No.

Do you want me to help you think of ways to make it right?

No. I'm mad at Bobby.

The child has to be willing to put forth effort or the amends become a crooked way to give a consequence. Teacher switches to the **Act** puzzle piece, takes Noah by the hand, leads him away from the easel, and gives the usual consequence.

Okay, Noah, you know the rules. Those who misuse the art area don't get to use it for the rest of the day. Find something else to do.

Amends should support family or classroom values. Suppose Noah thought of something he could do.

I could tear my painting.

Noah, in this classroom we take care of other people's property and our own.

Amends should help the child become a better person.

That wouldn't help you become a better person and it wouldn't fix Bobby's artwork. Can you think of something that would make it right for Bobby?

I could let him play with my truck, the one I brought from home.

The amends should be related to the problem.

You could, but that wouldn't fix the artwork. Can you think of something else?

No.

Do you want me to help you think of ways to make it right?

I guess so.

You could tape it with my help, or you could offer Bobby a new piece of paper, or you could make a wonderful picture of Bobby.

I'll give him the paper.

The amends made must be satisfactory to the victim.

Wait a minute. You need to find out if that would make it right for Bobby.

Bobby, here is a new piece of paper. Okay?

Not okay. I want you to fix this painting with tape.

Noah brought the tape and Teacher helped him do the job well. Teacher asks, *Okay Bobby?*

I guess so.

Noah, how do you feel about yourself now?

Noah grinned. *I'm still gonna let him play with my truck.*

Success! Bobby's need was addressed and Noah got to think of himself as competent instead of destructive.

There must be no resentment on parent's or teacher's part.

Teacher was pleased instead of irritated. If a parent or teacher who helps a child make amends feels resentful, the adult is probably too hurried, too tired, or doing too much of the work. In that case, use another puzzle piece and try making amends another day.

When children have had some practice making amends, sometimes they do it quickly.

Suppose the scenario had been about ridicule instead of damaged property. *Noah, when you laughed at Bobby's artwork you hurt his feelings. You know we have a no put-downs rule here. Do you want to make it up to him?* Noah thinks a while and says, *I'm sorry. Do you want to play with my truck? I'll get another truck and we can make a race track.* Bobby agrees and the incident is closed. Discipline lesson: If you do something wrong, you need to make it right.

Broken Promise

Aunt Nancy, the children's favorite, was arriving on a 12:30 flight. Because there had been an emergency at work, Mother needed to spend Saturday morning at the office and then drive directly to the airport. Mallory, nine, and Ian, twelve, were disappointed because they had looked forward to whooping and hollering when Aunt Nancy got off the plane. Well, okay, they decided they could plan a rackety greeting when she got out of the car. One problem solved.

The other problem was that Mother would not be there for Saturday morning chores. Mother, Ian, and Mallory made a list of what Mother could do Friday evening and what each child would do on Saturday. Great plan. Mother relaxed, sure that the children would do their parts.

Surprise! When Mother and Aunt Nancy arrived at the house, neither child was there to greet them and the house was a mess. As Mother alternated between worrying about where the children were and wanting to do them both serious bodily harm, the children screeched up on their bikes. They gave Aunt Nancy breathless hugs and explained to their mother that they were really, really sorry, but Chris had come by and told them there were clowns and a band at the park so they had gone over and really, really had planned to stay for only a short time, but they really, really had just forgotten about the time and they were really, really, really sorry.

Mother abandoned the idea of bodily harm, because she is against violence and anyway it would not remedy the situation. She asked that amends be made. She said sorry was fine and everyone makes mistakes, but what would they do to make it up to both her and Aunt Nancy? They did not know, but they guessed they could give Aunt Nancy whatever they had left of their allowances.

The amends made should be related to the problem.
Mother said, *That's an idea, but it doesn't fix the problem. You two go and think about what you can do to repair the situation. Then come and see if your plan is agreeable to me and would please Aunt Nancy.*

Making amends should help the child become a better person.

Think about how you want Aunt Nancy to view you.

Amends should support family or classroom values.

Right now she may think that people in our family don't keep promises and don't care about family members.

That's not true—we do care about her.

Okay, figure out how to put that into action.

Once the children were out of the room, Aunt Nancy graciously insisted that she really did not mind, that she loved them anyway, and that they were just kids. Mom responded firmly that it is the job of "just kids" to learn to be responsible and Aunt Nancy better help out with the process.

Mallory and Ian returned to ask if the women had already had lunch. The answer was no so the children made their proposal. *Mom, you take Aunt Nancy out for lunch, maybe a pretty long lunch, and when you come back, pretend you are just coming from the airport, but please call so we can tell you if it's okay to come home yet.*

The amends must be satisfactory to the victim.
Both Aunt Nancy and Mother thought this was a superb proposal.

The amender must put forth effort.
The children wolfed down sandwiches and hit the chores list. When Mother's car pulled up there was a *Welcome Aunt Nancy* banner on the front window and two children with bells and whistles. The house was orderly and the children had even

remembered to put the cleaning supplies away. Making amends worked wonderfully:

- Aunt Nancy was pleased.
- Mother was no longer resentful.
- The children extended effort, both to think of what to do and to do it.
- Making amends supported family values.
- The children's efforts were genuine.
- The amends did not encourage further offense.
- The children were proud of themselves. Their efforts had turned misbehavior into success.

Discipline lesson: Amends, well made, not only right the wrong, but build responsible children and enhance true self-esteem.

Damaged property and broken promises are not the only issues for which children can make amends. You might add parental worry, broken trust, a damaged reputation, broken curfew, stealing, cheating, lying. Choose examples based on your family's values.

> Making **Amends** is not about pain, but it is okay for children to experience the discomfort that is often an important part of learning.

References

[1] Gossen, Diane Chelsom. *Restitution: Restructuring School Discipline.* Chapel Hill, North Carolina: New View Publications, 1992.

8

Is There a Best Way to Put the Puzzle Pieces Together?

I can ask Philip to do something a hundred times and he never remembers. I'm so frustrated.

The best way to put the puzzle pieces together is the way that works for you and your family.

First remember the four options:

- **Attend** to the child, the situation, and yourself to get as much information as possible before you use the **Act, Ask,** or **Amend** puzzle pieces. Also teach the child to **Attend** to the outcomes of his behaviors.
- **Act** when a situation calls for immediate intervention or to prevent a misbehavior. You may **Act** to get a child's attention, to redirect behavior, or to allow a consequence that will teach a lesson.
- **Ask** to get information, to teach a child to listen, to teach a child to think, to encourage a child to act responsibly, to let a child know you are attempting to understand his point of view.
- Make **Amends** to rebuild connection with a child whom you have slighted or wronged. Teach a child to make **Amends** to help the child right a wrong and help the child build positive attitudes and behavior patterns.

Then choose the puzzle piece that is most likely to be effective. If you are especially good at observing, you can **Attend** and then decide if you need to **Ask** or **Act**. Sometimes when we pause to attend we realize that this is a problem that children can resolve for themselves.

If your child is wiggly and learns most quickly when his body is moving, you will probably start with **Act.** Also, when a child tends not to listen, action usually works best.

Maybe your child lacks empathy for the people she has inconvenienced or hurt. Then, whenever you have the time, energy, and patience to make sure she completes her restitution, you will start with making **Amends**.

When a child has been lazy about thinking, you can **Ask** not just one but a whole series of questions that challenge the child to think.

Follow these four steps for using Time-In discipline:

1. Stop the unwanted behavior.
2. Ask yourself, *What does the child need to learn about this?*
3. Use the puzzle pieces in any order or any combination.
4. Notice the pieces that this particular child responds to. Use those rather than the ones you personally would respond to.

> Remember, whenever you can resolve a discipline problem with one puzzle piece you are keeping your discipline short and effective, but there is no magic formula that always works.

9

What if Time-In Doesn't Work?

When Time-In isn't working, I need Time-Out!

What if you have been using Time-In and the children's behavior does not improve, or, oh woe, seems to be worse instead of better? If you have just started using Time-In, remember that children often increase their misbehaviors when grown-ups change their way of disciplining. Children test us to be sure we really mean to follow the new way, and some kids are expert testers!

However, the misbehavior could be for one of three other reasons:

- The misbehavior may be a symptom of another problem in the child's life.
- Right now in your life it may be hard for you to stay calm and consistent in the face of misbehavior.
- Time-In deals with misbehavior and strengthens the bonds in the family, but it may not get at the cause of the misbehavior.

Problems in the Child's Life

If you suspect there is something else going on in the child's life, start with *health.* A child who is not getting enough sleep, does not eat well, does not feel well, or cannot see or hear well, will often engage in disruptive behavior. Sometimes these children do not know why they are misbehaving. *Little Jana was allergic to wool and feathers and would not stay in her bed. What her parents saw as willfulness was little Jana's attempt to find a place where she could sleep.*

Check the child's stress level. Young children who have a schedule that requires more transitions than they can handle often get very fussy.[1] Older children who are overscheduled sometimes become very self-centered: *"Drive me now!"*[2]

Introverted children need free time to refuel their batteries. Extroverted children can nag when they do not have enough people stimulation.

Too much television stresses children of any age because they are not moving their bodies enough. Besides, the programs they watch often show them how to strike before they think and lead to a lack of the creativity that is crucial for problem solving.

If the behavior parents expect is too advanced for the child's age or capability, children can become hopeless or surly. Or, if parents do things for the child that he is ready to learn for himself, the child may become edgy or demanding.[3] Sometimes children are sad, angry, embarrassed, frustrated, or confused about something the parents do not connect with the misbehavior or do not know about:

- Libby, four, was sad and confused when her older sister started school. Libby started wetting her pants and breaking things.
- The parents of five-year-old Jeff's friend were getting a divorce and Jeff, afraid his parents would separate, "blew up" whenever his parents had a disagreement.
- Seven-year-old Emma was terrified of a bully at school who threatened to beat her up if she told. Emma dawdled in the morning and often missed her school bus.
- Twelve-year-old Hayden was threatened by armed gang members. He skipped school, came home at odd times, and his grades dropped.

Each of these children needs help and as long as their parents look only at the behavior, not at what is behind it, the misbehavior will probably continue until the underlying cause is addressed.

Stresses in the Family

Conflicts between family members may be difficult to resolve because parents need better conflict resolution skills.[4] If parents unwittingly show favoritism or deliberately set up competition for love and attention within the family, children will push to get the attention they need through misbehavior. Remember, children need to feel recognized and connected, so negative attention is better than no attention at all.

Sometimes there is stress in the family (illness, job loss, addiction, divorce, etc.). Children know when something stressful is going on, even if the adults do not talk about it or insist it is not a big deal. Children often express stress for the family by doing things that are hurtful and disruptive and look dumb. Parents need to attend to stressors in the family. That is the job of the grown-ups.

Parents Need Support or Relief

If it takes a village to raise a child, many of us are saying, *Where is my village? Where is the support I need? I haven't had the patience or energy to enforce the rules, so my child doesn't believe he has to follow them, and I have been criticizing and punishing.* Or we say, *Other adults let children be rude and get away with anything. My children think I'm weird.*

Yes, much of the American adult world gives in to children or views them as a "market segment" rather than as young human beings who need years of love and training in order to become adults who are responsible for themselves and to others. At this time, good parenting is a counterculture activity. It is not surprising, therefore, that parents often feel stressed and alone.

> We need to remember that good parenting is not a popularity contest. It is offering children the life lessons they need.

Since love and the important lessons of discipline are the best gifts parents can give to children, find some ways to get your needs met so you can give those gifts.

References

[1]Brazelton, T. Berry, M.D. *Touchpoints, The Essential Reference: Your Child's Emotional and Behavioral Development.* Reading, Mass.: Addison-Wesley Publishing Co., Inc., 1992. Has extensive information on handling transitions.

[2]Doherty, William J., Ph.D. *The Intentional Family: How to Build Family Ties in Our Modern World.* Reading, Mass.: Addison-Wesley Publishing Co., Inc., 1997. Good for ideas about putting balance in the family schedule and creating rituals that stabilize the family.

[3]Clarke, Jean Illsley and Connie Dawson. *Growing Up Again: Parenting Ourselves, Parenting Our Children.* 2nd edition. Center City, Minn.: Hazelden, 1998. See the section on overindulgence.

[4]Crary, Elizabeth. *Help! The Kids Are at It Again: Using Kid's Quarrels to Teach "People" Skills.* Seattle, Wash.: Parenting Press, Inc., 1997.

10

What if My Anger Gets in the Way?

But what about my anger? I think I understand Time-In, but I get so angry when my child pulls the same old tricks! I can't stay positive.

Who among us has not felt anger, despair, or even rage when we have done the best we could, have other worries, and are probably tired, hungry, and in need of recreation or love ourselves?[1]

Well, we all know about anger management—take ten deep breaths, beat on a pillow, go for a walk, or take a relaxing bath, etc. But if we are trying to use Time-In with a child who has been pushing our anger buttons all day, ten deep breaths do not make a dent. If we are dealing with a kid who just smashed a vase or hit her brother, it is hardly the time to stop and beat on a pillow. If we have a child who has just run away, this is not the time for a long walk. If the youngster just tried to drown the gerbil, a relaxing bath simply does not fit.

What Anger Can Teach Us

Anger is always a sign that there is something that we want to keep or to change. The thing we want to keep may be threatened or we may feel powerless to change the thing we want to change. When I want to change a noisy, tantrum-filled house to one of peace and quiet and I cannot succeed in doing that, it is normal, natural, and appropriate for me to feel angry. My anger is a signal to myself that I need to pay attention to my needs. Maybe I have to get an hour of peace and quiet somewhere else. Maybe I need to look at my rules about peace and quiet—do I really need it or do I think it is the sign of a successful parent? Maybe I need to learn some new parenting skills and give up the wish that a new skill will work immediately. Or I may need to accept that my kid is wired on fast forward and learn how to deal with that *and* take care of myself at the same time.

Here are five things you can do to put your anger to work helping you:

- Look at the list of reasons why kids may be misbehaving (see chapter 9). If there is an underlying cause, go to work on that. It is worth the effort for your child and for your peace of mind.
- Remember that what works for you and your child may not be what your friend or your sister or your neighbor thinks you should do. Turn off criticism and shame and think of one thing you can do that will help you feel better and will help solve the problem.
- Find some sympathetic, non-blaming support for yourself. Find a good counselor if you need one. Like an abscessed

tooth, for which you need to see the dentist, you may have an old anger you are not even aware of that is spilling out into your behavior and onto your child.

- If the child's misbehavior is a big, serious offense, breathe deeply, center yourself, and use the energy from your anger to find help.
- If the misbehavior is "normal kid stuff," laugh at your own intensity.

> Do not laugh at the child's misbehavior—that will increase it.

Laugh at the fact that children have been perplexing and bugging their parents forever, and your child is no different. Celebrate the wonderfulness that your children have you around to insist that they learn lessons of good behavior. Choose the discipline that teaches the lesson your child needs and wish yourself good luck. Thank your anger for telling you that your child did something and now you need to do something.

If you do not feel angry, but are tired, listless, hopeless, and depressed, consider that you may have some anger turned inward. In that case, recognizing the anger and taking action to improve the situation can help restore your health and energy.

> Your anger is your friend. It is a signal that it is time to take action to change what you want to change or to keep what you want to keep.

References

[1]Lerner, Harriet Goldhur. *The Dance of Anger.* New York: HarperCollins, 1985. Helpful information for understanding anger.

Conclusion: What Else Can a Parent Do?

When no discipline seems to work, remember that sometimes a child just feels contrary on a particular day. We adults also have days when we "got up on the wrong side of the bed."

There are, however, four things parents can do to improve the outcome of discipline.

First, refocus on your own values. Think about what you really want for your children and then ask yourself if that is what your discipline is teaching.

Second, check yourself to make sure you are not giving contradictory messages such as, *I'll do that for you/why don't you know how to do that?* Conflicting messages create double binds and double binds are confusing for children. Also, make sure you are not smiling at misbehavior. Children will do most anything that parents smile at.

Third, remember that you are an important influence on your child's life, and there are many other influences as well. When your child is surrounded by pressures that encourage self-centeredness and instant gratification and you feel as if your voice is a dim call in the wilderness, find a way, at least once a month, to push back on the culture. Feel free! The culture pushes on you all of the time! Write a letter to a television station. Visit your child's school. Write a letter to the newspaper editor. Form a block group. Join a parenting class or group to find others who share your values.

Fourth, somehow, some way, take better care of yourself. **Attend** to yourself as well as your children. Eat less junk food. Lower the noise level in your home. Turn off the television. Demand that the children pay attention to you. Find some way to keep the children safe while you have a Time-Out when you need it! Remember times when you have parented well, take a deep breath, and wind up the courage to be the parent you want to be. Your children will respect you for it. And they will make whatever decisions they make about their experiences.

> Parents are responsible for the discipline process. Children are responsible for the outcome.

Encourage yourself to do the best you can each day and start the next day with love and hope. Stay connected with your children and remember that you are your children's best gift. Celebrate that.

Index

Other Books and Materials

Connections: The Threads That Strengthen Families by Jean Illsley Clarke. Center City, Minn.: Hazelden, 1999. $16.95

Growing Up Again: Parenting Ourselves, Parenting Our Children by Jean Illsley Clarke and Connie Dawson. 2nd edition. Center City, Minn.: Hazelden, 1998. $16.95

Growing Up Again Leader's Guide by Jean Illsley Clarke. Available from Parenting Press, www.ParentingPress.com

How Much Is Enough? Everything You Need to Know to Steer Clear of Overindulgence and Raise Likeable, Responsible, and Respectful Children by Jean Illsley Clarke, Connie Dawson, and David Bredehoft. New York: Marlowe and Co., 2004. $14.95

How Much Is Enough Leader's Guide by Jean Illsley Clarke. Available from Parenting Press, www.ParentingPress.com

Self-Esteem: A Family Affair by Jean Illsley Clarke. 2nd edition. Center City, Minn.: Hazelden, 1998. $16.00

Who, Me Lead a Group? By Jean Illsley Clarke. Seattle: Parenting Press, 1998. $9.95

Write to Daisy Press, 16535 Ninth Avenue North, Minneapolis, MN 55447 for ordering information on the following materials.

Affirmation Ovals. Colored and laminated ovals available as bookmarks and in pocket, table, and wall sizes. Each set includes developmental affirmations for nine stages of growth.

Affirmation Ovals: 139 Ways to Give and Get Affirmations by Jean Illsley Clarke and Carole Gesme. A book of games and activities to help people of all ages use developmental affirmation ovals.

The Important Infants (birth to six months), *The Wonderful Busy Ones* (6 months to 18 months), *The Terrific Twos* (18 months to 3 years) by Jean Illsley Clarke. Audio cassette tapes presenting important information about children and the nurturing they need.

Sing Yes! by Darrell Faires. Six audio cassette tapes containing 63 singable and easy-to-remember songs based on developmental affirmations.

Ups & Downs with Feelings, The Love Game, The Family Puzzle: Putting the Pieces Together, Capture a Feeling, and *Keyed Up for Being Drug-Free* by Carole Gesme. Games that support growing up again and building self-esteem.

Skill-building books for parents from Parenting Press, Inc.

Without Spanking or Spoiling: A Practical Approach to Toddler and Preschool Guidance by Elizabeth Crary takes the best ideas from four major child guidance approaches and combines them into one practical resource guide. Useful with ages birth to 6 years. 112 pages, $14.95 paper, $19.95 library binding

Pick Up Your Socks . . . and Other Skills Growing Children Need! by Elizabeth Crary shows parents how to teach responsibility. A job chart listing average ages kids do household chores helps reduce unrealistic expectations. Useful with ages 3 to 12 years. 112 pages, $14.95 paper, $19.95 library binding

Help! The Kids Are at It Again: Using Kid's Quarrels to Teach "People" Skills by Elizabeth Crary shows parents how to make peace in their families. Children need to learn social skills and parents can teach them with the help of this practical, wise book. Useful with all ages. 96 pages, $11.95 paper, $18.95 library binding

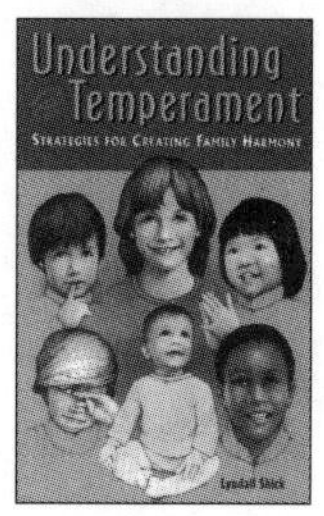

Understanding Temperament: Strategies for Creating Family Harmony by Lyndall Shick, M.A. is a guide to behavior based in temperament. Parents teach skills children need to excel in the world, break the cycle of negative behavior between parent and child, and solve problems by improving the "fit"between child and environment. Useful with all ages. 126 pages, $13.95 paper, $19.95 library binding

Temperament Tools: Working with Your Child's Inborn Traits by Helen Neville, R.N. and Diane Clark Johnson helps parents deal with the behavior problems that are common to children of certain temperament types. Useful with birth to 5 years. 128 pages, $13.95 paper, $19.95 library binding

Redirecting Children's Behavior, 3rd edition, revised, by Kathryn Kvols examines reasons children misbehave and offers parents tried-and-true ways to foster closeness, cooperation, and respect in their families. Useful with ages birth to 18 years. 176 pages, $14.95 paper, $19.95 library binding

Grounded for Life?! Stop Blowing Your Fuse and Start Communicating with Your Teenager by Louise Felton Tracy, M.A. shows parents how to communicate effectively and avoid problems with their children. *Parents' Choice* award winner. Useful with ages 10 to 18 years. 164 pages, $14.95 paper, $19.95 library binding

---